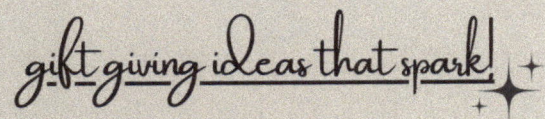 

Welcome

Greetings and welcome! Thank you for taking your valuable time to elevate your gift-giving game.

Before we dive in, pause for a moment and think about the best gift you've ever received. One that surprised you. One you didn't see coming. I bet it made you feel loved, seen, and deeply appreciated. Maybe your whole day changed because of it. Maybe your whole mood changed. And I'm willing to bet your view of the person who gave it to you shifted in a positive, lasting way.

You experienced the joy of being truly gifted.

Now let me ask you this: have you ever created that feeling for someone else?

Do you want to become the kind of gifter who can?

Because gifting isn't just about exchanging things...it's about connection. A well-chosen gift can say:

I see you. I know you. You matter to me. I care.

Gift giving is powerful. It's one of the five recognized love languages. It can open hearts, shift perspectives, and deepen bonds. The right gift feels like a warm embrace, like grandma's sweet potato pie, like making the winning basket. It brings joy. It creates memories. It builds relationships.

But let's be honest: not all gifts make the mark.

We've all received the random socks, the itchy sweater, the item that felt like an afterthought. Gifts like that tend to fade into the background... forgettable and unremarkable. And here's the thing: that doesn't mean the gifter didn't care. Most people put in effort. They think of you, shop around, wrap it up, show up, and present it with a smile. But somewhere along the way, the spark gets lost.

That's where this book steps in.

This guide is here to help you reconnect with the heart of gifting. To give you tools, inspiration, and simple strategies to make every gift count. Whether you're celebrating a birthday, holiday, milestone, or just want to say "I thought of you." This book will help you do it with intention and joy.

Let's make gifting meaningful again. Let's make it fun. Let's make it unforgettable. Ready? Let's begin.

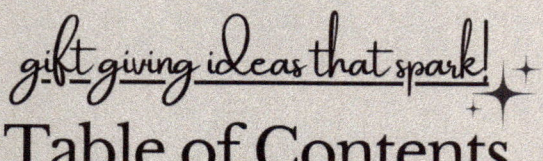

gift giving ideas that spark!

Table of Contents

Welcome	1
Table of Contents	2
Gifter's Mindset	3
Purpose of a Gift	4-5
Gift Rules	6
Relationship Dynamics	7
Pros and Cons	8
Prompted Activity	9
Personalization Tips	10-11
Common Mistakes	12
Gift Planning Tippers	13
Thoughtful Gift List	14
A Gift Story	15
Let's Reflect	16
With Appreciation	17
Parting Gifts	18-23
About the Author	24

gift giving ideas that spark! ✦

Gifter's Mindset

Let's jump in! Below are the core beliefs and habits that shape a gifter's mindset:

1. Connectivity: "I pay attention." You believe in observing people's lives, what they love, what excites them, what they need but never ask for. You're tuned in and emotionally present.

2. Creativity: "I'm willing to think differently." You don't default towards generic solutions. You ask: What would make this feel special or unexpected? Your mindset values originality, even in what someone would consider the simplest gestures.

3. Caring: "I give because I care, not because I have to." You see gifting as a form of love or respect...not a social obligation. That's why your gifts carry emotional weight.

4. Willingness: "I go the extra mile." You're not afraid of effort. You'll research, personalize, or plan to make someone feel truly seen. You're willing to do what others won't.

5. Focus: "I give with clarity, not convenience." Instead of rushing, you slow down to be intentional. You ask: What do they need? What would bring them joy right now? Your choices come from insight, not impulse.

6. Thought: "I give with purpose." Every gift has a reason. You're thoughtful about timing, message, and meaning. The result? A gift that feels right because it's grounded in real care.

7. Time: "Time invested is love shown." You understand that great gifts take time: time in planning, time in simply noticing someone's needs, and time to purchase and prepare the gift. Don't rush the process.

8. Effort: "My energy is part of the gift." The care you put into the presentation of the gift. Also depending on the gift, how it's delivered is part of the experience. Effort communicates value.

It is about being deliberate and emotionally aware, not about perfection, but presence.

The Purpose of a Gift

At its core, the purpose of a gift is to express deeply something your connection to someone. It shows love, appreciation, and value and that you value the giftee. It says:
That I see you. I thought of you. I care.

A gift is a tangible and meaningful way to reflect our ability to connect with others. It's not just about the item in the bag or the wrapping on the box. It's about the connection that lives underneath it.

Whether you're placing a few dollars into the guitar case of a street musician, wrapping a blanket for a newborn baby, or honoring beautiful (and challenging) years of marriage, the heart behind every gift is the same:

We are connected. And this is how I show it.

Gifting, when done with intention, becomes more than a tradition or social norm; it becomes a language of celebration, compassion, and love. When you understand this, the idea of "just picking something up" begins to shift.

It's not about the price.

It's not about perfection.

It's about the presence behind the gesture.

The sweetest gifts are given simply because someone crossed your mind.
The most thoughtful gifts come from a place of genuine care.
And the most heartfelt gifts are rooted deeply in love.

 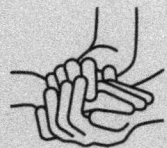 

No matter the moment, a milestone or just because, when you give with purpose, your gift becomes more. It evolves into a message that speaks to the heart.

You matter. I thought of you. You are not alone.

And in today's world, that kind of connection is a gift.

Below is a visual centered on the giftee, they are being celebrated and the gift expresses the connection. This highlights how important they are to you as the gifter. At its core, it's all about the relationship.

I'm **Proud of You**

Congrats!

Take advantage of opportunities to connect...

Celebrate and Connect

Don't miss opportunities to make your gift spark!

thinking of you

House Warming

Bar Mitzvah

Mis 15 Años

You **Did It!**

gift giving ideas that spark!

Gift Rules

It is easy to be a lackluster gift giver. It happens with no ill intent. Life gets in the way. We are all so busy. It is not realistic to make every gift meaningful. Or is it? Following the rules will improve your intentional gifter skills.

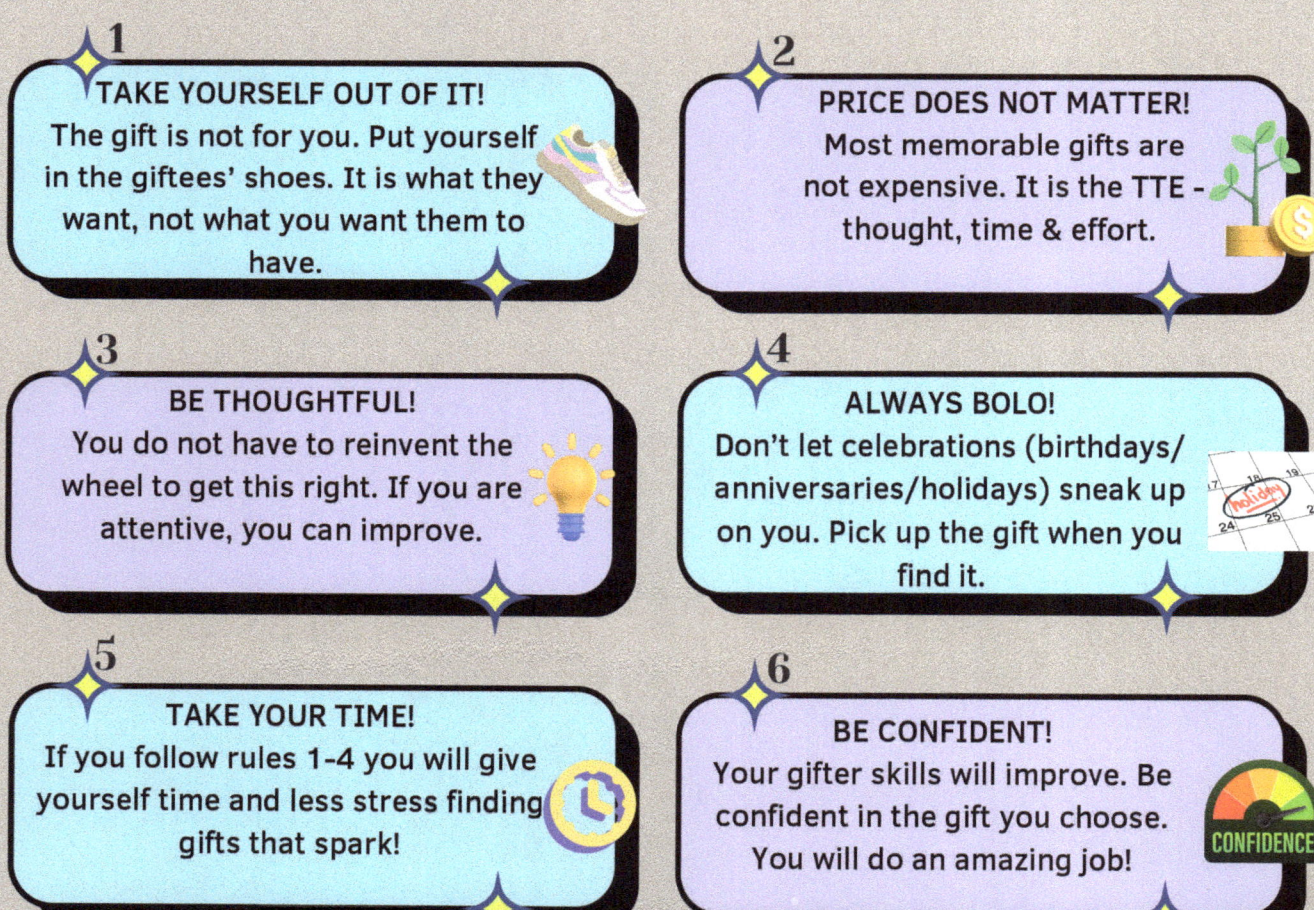

1

TAKE YOURSELF OUT OF IT!
The gift is not for you. Put yourself in the giftees' shoes. It is what they want, not what you want them to have.

2

PRICE DOES NOT MATTER!
Most memorable gifts are not expensive. It is the TTE - thought, time & effort.

3

BE THOUGHTFUL!
You do not have to reinvent the wheel to get this right. If you are attentive, you can improve.

4

ALWAYS BOLO!
Don't let celebrations (birthdays/ anniversaries/holidays) sneak up on you. Pick up the gift when you find it.

5

TAKE YOUR TIME!
If you follow rules 1-4 you will give yourself time and less stress finding gifts that spark!

6

BE CONFIDENT!
Your gifter skills will improve. Be confident in the gift you choose. You will do an amazing job!

gift giving ideas that spark!

Relationship Dynamics

💡 Think of a person from your professional and personal relationships. List three gifts you think they would enjoy and why. Do not think of an event or occasion, just the person. There's space on the last page of the book for notes.

PROFESSIONAL
VERSUS
Personal

Professional paraphernalia, collector items	Anticipate the expectation and exceed the expectation
Purchase as a group and present during an event	Personal relationships require work - make the gift stackable- this means having additional smaller gifts or an activity planned to heighten the reception of the gift
Understand the recipient and the occasion to determine formal or informal type of gift and/or event to present the gift	Timing and presentation are everything (always TTE)
Follow legal and ethical guidelines concerning costs and other restrictions	Relate gift to an experience or conversation

gift giving ideas that spark! ✦

Pros and Cons Gift Planner List

Let's be clear: there are no cons in becoming an intentional gifter. However, there are a few do's and don'ts.

DO

1. Plan. Know your budget and gift options.
2. Understand your relationship status.
3. Create stackables when possible.
4. Presentation matters, cater to the giftee.

Pro: Make this gift intentional. Doing this shows you are truly connected with the giftee.

DON'T

1. Wait. Plan and purchase in advance.
2. Overspend. Gift giving is not about the money, it is about care and concern.
3. Take the easy route. Find a gift that sparks!

Pro: In the end you won't be rushed, and you will have the time to find a gift from the heart. It takes thought, time and effort-TTE.

gift giving ideas that spark!
Prompted Activity

You may not say it out loud, but some gifts are blah, lackluster, forgettable. Let these moments stay with you and shape how you give moving forward.

Take a few moments to think back on your own experiences. Let's explore three specific gifts that missed the mark and why. Write down those three specific gifts and, one on each page. If you are having trouble, think of the following:

1. A gift that you regifted
2. A gift that went unused
3. A gift you discarded or donated

What made the gift miss the mark? Did you feel like someone thought of you when the gift was purchased. Do you feel they just missed the mark?

Personalization Tips

Don't be cheesy, unless it is the right type of cheese for the occasion. Most items can be personalized, that doesn't mean that all items should be personalized.

Know the person well. Ask the question, will this stay in the box or be on display? Is this one-time wear or something that can be used again?

When done right, you realize: "This isn't just a gift. This is you, through my eyes. I wanted you to feel remembered."

That's why people save them. That's why it elicits emotion when they open them. That's why they don't throw them away, even years later. They become forever keepsakes.

Not every moment needs a custom-made item. And not every person wants to wear the matching tee shirt, or to display an engraved plaque. Sometimes, what you believe is thoughtful may feel awkward or uncomfortable for the giftee.

The most important rule comes into play: know your giftee.

When you get it right, a personalized gift can become one of the most treasured possessions someone owns and not because of its cost, but because of the connection it represents. It becomes a bookmark in their story.

A reminder that they were seen, heard, known, and celebrated in a way that no one else could replicate.

11

gift giving ideas that spark!

Common Mistakes

- Sorry, I missed the mark.

- I forgot the gift. This was obviously not your greatest moment.

- I regifted an old unwanted gift.

- I asked someone else to pick something up for me. You may get lucky.

- I added my name to the gift...I will be just as surprised as the person receiving the gift!

- I did not read the exchange rules for price and was below the price point.

- I did not have the gift prepared. No wrapping paper, gift bag, or tissue paper.

- My presentation was regifted or worn. Please have a fresh gift presentation.

- Although I tried, it looked like I didn't care because I was last minute. This one feels bad.

- The dog ate it, or any other excuse you make up to avoid the fact you did not have a gift.

Being a gifter comes from the heart. You are someone who finds joy in celebrating others with meaning and care. Most people want loved ones to know and feel they love them; gifts are a medium. Yes, these are easy ways to miss the mark, everyone has experienced more items on this list than they care to admit. It is time, put forth the TTE, thought, time, and effort to turn over a new leaf. 🌱

gift giving ideas that spark!

Gift Planning Tippers

Here are a few tippers to keep in mind when choosing a truly memorable gift.

💮 1. Know the Giftee Deeply: What are their current interests, obsessions, hobbies? Have they hinted at anything recently, even casually? Are they more practical or sentimental? What makes them smile, light up, or laugh in conversation.

💬 2. Consider the Occasion: Is this a milestone? A personal celebration? A professional thank-you? Should the gift be public or private? Is this a "standalone" gift, part of a shared experience or a stackable?

❤️ 3. Add Meaning, Not Just Money: The best gifts don't have to be expensive, they have to be personal. A small, thoughtful item with a handwritten note often leaves more impact than a luxury item with no story. Look for opportunities to use the "inside jokes" or shared memories to create an intentional gifter opportunity.

🕵️ 4. Observe & Listen: Pay attention to what the giftee says, "in passing" or "one day I'll..." Notice what they surround themselves with what colors, brands, books, decor. What's something they always give to others but never buy for themselves?

✏️ 5. Make It Feel Like a Surprise, Not an Obligation: Sometimes you can skip the Wishlist and deliver the unexpected in a beautiful way. Don't ask what they want, notice what they need or what would uplift them.

🍀 6. Consider Gifting Experiences or Customizations: Memory making gifts (spa day, cooking class, custom art, name engraving, etc.) feel unforgettable. Combine something tangible with something emotional (e.g. a framed photo + a note) ...create a stackable.

📝 7. Take Notes Year-Round: Keep a running list of gift ideas in a notebook or phone. Great gifting is easier when it's not the last minute. Check out my interactive intentional gifter journal as well, until then take good notes.

💡Pro Tip: If the gift feels like a reflection of your relationship,
pat yourself on the back. It's the right one.

gift giving ideas that spark!
Thoughtful Gift List

Every gift should be given with TTE -thought, time and effort. But the greatest of these is the thought. At the end of this guide, you will be given space and time to brainstorm for future gifter opportunities. I hope that you are already thinking of wonderful ways you can show how much you care and bring the spark into your giving. Keep an open list of thoughtful gifts for the people who are near and dear to you. This takes time and effort, but it is well worth it.

First consider the giftee - what they would want for themselves but may not buy or take time out for themselves. For instance, a good friend going through a stressful time you may want to treat them to a massage. What a thoughtful gift.

You can increase the spark with stackables and through presentation: A wrapped box with a handwritten note, decadent chocolates, rooibos tea and honey.

To further heighten this gift, you can add the element of surprise and schedule the massage. Invite your friend to grab a bit, present the gift. The surprise is that a massage is next. Have the massage scheduled after you eat. As a bonus, treat yourself too!

A Gift Story

I am a member of my local yoga studio, and I absolutely love my kind and welcoming community. I value and respect my yoga instructors; they are pure joy. December the studios celebrates its' anniversary and there's the bonus that it's Christmas time. For me December represents so many positive things, especially the season of giving. I cheerfully give each instructor a gift. I have given candles, journals and a curated essential oil blend over the years. What I would call lump gifts. Every year I receive the same response. Thank you and you're so thoughtful.

This past year I was online looking for blankies to donate to cancer patients for my sorority's cancer care drive. I love good throws, blankies, blankets.... covers period. So, I ordered a couple to donate. Once they arrived, I opened one to feel the softness and I loved it. This has a point, I promise. Just work with me.

I immediately thought of my amazing yoga instructors. You see, at my yoga studio I am affectionally known as the blanket yogi. I bundle up in the coziest savasana during each practice. One day an instructor grabbed one of my blankets to tuck me in. I shared with her later that the blanket was my grandma's blanket and it is my most sentimental possession. Long story short: all the instructors were gifted blankets. A gift they could directly link to me and know how much I love blankets are why my yoga blanket is so special to me.

Then I turned it into a stackable: I presented a picture of me doing a tree pose during my travels. Then on the back of the photo, I wrote each of them a personal handwritten note, intentionally including something special about them that resonates with me.

Their response was overwhelming to my heart. I received return handwritten notes, one instructor told me the note brought her to tears, and I received a plethora of welcomed hugs. I am glad I expressed how much I care about them.

Intentional Gifter: IG/TikTok/FB page, let's connect.

Let's Reflect

1. Finding your why?
It's all about connecting with others
Being an intentional gifter is knowing it is not just an exchange, it is showing someone you see them and you care. Remember this guide is to change your relationship from being a mundane gift giver to being a far more intentional gifter.

2. Gifts are not about the price. Ultimately you convey your thoughtfulness and care by being attentive and giving from your heart.
Your new relationship with gift giving has new terms:

Gifter
Stackables
TTE - Thought, Time, and Effort

3. Gift giving as an intentional gifter begins and ends with the person receiving the gift. It's not about the price tag, popularity of the item, or even the occasion; it's about the person. A truly meaningful gift is one that reflects a deep understanding of who they are, what they value, and how they experience the world.

"You want to communicate their importance in your life."

Your gift is a message. It says, "I see you. I know you. You matter to me." Whether spoken or silent, the act of giving is an opportunity to express gratitude, love, appreciation, or respect. The more thought you invest in choosing something that resonates with their personality, dreams, or memories, the more your gift becomes a symbol of your relationship.

gift giving ideas that spark!

With Appreciation

I want to express my deepest appreciation to you for being a part of this journey. While this may be the first time I've shared my intentional gifter passion publicly, this path is one I've truly been on my entire life.

I am an intentional gifter by nature. I will pick up a gift for someone I love at any time, for any reason, because the people I care about are always on my mind and in my heart. That part comes effortlessly to me. But the true labor of love is in the intention and the TTE, the thought, time, and effort it takes to figure out... what will genuinely bring someone joy? What will stir their heart? What will make them feel seen, known, and loved, without a single word? That's the art of giving. And that's what I've poured into this guide.

You're now part of the very beginning of something near and dear to me. I can't thank you enough for reading, for caring and for being willing to grow as or into an intentional gifter.

My hope is that this guide helps you give gifts that carry the sincerity of your thoughts and the warmth of your heart. May your gifts reflect the love behind them.

This is just the beginning.... You're reading the first in a series of intentional gifter publications. I hope this guide and future books refreshes the way you process gift giving and awaken the intentional gifter in you.

I'd love to hear your gift ideas and stories. Please share them with me using the QR code on page 24 and let's keep inspiring each other to give with intention.

17

Parting Gifts (my fav-stackables...)

What kind of Gifter's Guide would this be if I didn't leave you with a gift?
As any true gifter knows, a well-rounded gift is all about the extras, the thoughtful touches, the follow-up moments...what I call stackables. The next few pages are filled with some helpful fun interactive insight, because meaningful gifting is layered.
These five "stackables" are like the bonus gifts you didn't expect, but you love and use time and time again as you become a more intentional gifter.

🎁 Stackable 1: The Brainstorming Exercise
Think before you gift. Here you'll find a guided prompt to help you identify three real people, personal and professional, and brainstorm meaningful gifts using the techniques from this guide. Think: relationship + occasion + impact.

✉️ Stackable 2: The Power of the Handwritten Note
A timeless keepsake. This section revisits the underrated power of a handwritten letter and gives you suggestions for what to include in one.

⚠️ Stackable 3: The Easy Way Out
Why gift cards and money are great, but they can be better. You'll explore how to make the "easy way out" feel thoughtful.

🔖 Stackable 4: Stackables Defined
What is a stackable? Here, you'll learn how to create layered gift experiences... pairing physical gifts with emotional touches like a note, a playlist, or an experience. These are the gifts people remember.

💡 Stackable 5: "Gifter" Defined
A mindset, not a title. In this final section, I provide a visual definition of an "Intentional Gifter," someone who uses intention to connect and celebrate the care within a relationship. Whether your gift is tangible or intangible, simple or elaborate, this is the 'visual' identity of your mindset in becoming an intentional gifter.

18

S1 - Brainstorm

Now that you understand the fundamentals of an intentional gifter, it's time to apply what you've learned.

Choose three people (it doesn't matter if they are personal, or professional or a combination) whom you plan to give a gift to soon, within the next 60 days. Be specific and intentional in your choices. Think about upcoming birthdays, anniversaries, milestones, or even "just because" moments. It may feel easier to start personal relationships because someone always has an upcoming occasion. Also pay attention to the impact that a well-chosen professional gift can make.

Let's be honest, as time goes on, shopping for our loved ones becomes more challenging. We've celebrated with them for years. We've gifted them all the "obvious" things. So, out of convenience, we may fall back on gift cards or cash. And while those gifts can absolutely be appreciated, especially when they're needed, it doesn't reflect the connection of your relationship.

A thoughtful gift, on the other hand, carries a message. It conveys to the giftee: "I paid attention. I remembered. I wanted this to reflect you." That's what makes it unforgettable.

✍️Your Gifting Exercise

- Write down three names of people you'd like to give a gift to soon.
- Use the Gift Rules (pg. 6) and other helpful advice in this guide. Also understand the relationship, know their tastes, consider the occasion, respect boundaries, and prioritize meaning.
- Brainstorm possible gift ideas for each person. Think beyond the generic and mundane. What would make them feel seen?

S2 The handwritten note effect...

✉️ The Underrated Power of a Handwritten Note

Don't underestimate the quiet strength of a handwritten note, card, or letter. Among all the gifts you could possibly give, this is one of the most powerful. It doesn't require wrapping paper, a receipt, or a shipping label. But what it does carry is immeasurable: emotion, memory, and presence.

A handwritten message gives you the rare opportunity to speak love, light, and life into someone... whether it's a cherished friend, a partner, a mentor, or a respected colleague. It's the kind of gift that becomes a keepsake, not because of its cost, but because of its value. Years later, these words may still be folded in a drawer, tucked in a wallet, or pressed between pages of a book. It's also the perfect stackable, the kind of gift you can pair with something tangible or not. In this digital age, you can also take a picture of the note and send via text or email.

💌 What to Include in a Meaningful Note

- Say "I love you." Some people don't hear this enough. Writing it down means they can revisit your words any time they need to feel seen and remembered.

- Express what they mean to you. Be specific... mention their impact. Let them know they are valued, not for what they do, but for who they are.

- Share your gratitude. Reflect on how they've enriched your life. Say the things you don't always say out loud. "I can't imagine life without you" hits differently when it's in ink.

S3 The easy way out

1

$CASH$
Convenient, immediate just transfer the funds, but lacks a personal touch. Still send the CASHAPP and create a stackable!

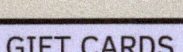

2

GIFT CARDS
Have the same effect as cash. However, many gift cards are lost and never used, electronic gift cards are more convenient and safer.

GIFT CARD

3

PHONE A FRIEND
It's good to recognize you need help and it is better than not taking the initiative. But don't overly rely on others because you're the gifter.

To add a personal touch to cash and gift cards, add a handwritten or digital card with a personal note. Sometimes we can't be there in person, and you may have time constraints with shipping. It happens and these options are easy, the key is to make them stackables. Stackables allows the gift (and funds) to keep giving with intention.

S4 Define stackables?

STACKABLES MAKE GIFTS SPARK!

WHAT ARE STACKABLE GIFTS?

Stackables are those priceless bonus elements that elevate a gift from thoughtful to unforgettable.

VERSATILITY

Stackables are unique additions that are expressive, experiential, or practical. This makes the gift feel layered and personal.

BENEFITS

Stackables connect the layers of the relationship They bring value to the gift exchange because they reflect a memory, bring meaning, and context. Priceless.

🎁 **1. Handwritten Note or Letter**
A heartfelt message instantly adds meaning. Pairing a physical gift with a handwritten card or letter gives emotional depth and often becomes the part of the gift people keep longest.
Example: A book + a letter explaining why this story reminded you of them.

🎶 **2. Custom Playlist or QR Code to a Memory**
Music triggers memory and emotion. A curated playlist tied to your relationship, or the moment makes the gift feel connection.
Example: A framed photo + a QR code to a playlist of "your songs" or a shared memory soundtrack.

🧡 **3. Personal Token or Symbol**
Include something symbolic that ties into the gift or relationship. A pressed flower, a charm, a photo strip, or a memento that means something only to the two of you.
Example: A cozy blanket + a keychain engraved with "home" for someone moving far away.

📖 **4. Mini Experience or Prompt**
Give the giftee something to do with the gift. This could be an invitation, a recipe, a challenge, or a candle making class.
Example: A specialty mug + a hot cocoa mix + a card that says "This is for our first snow day" + a recipe or quote.

S5 Define gifter?

Hopefully, by now, you see yourself in a refreshed light as someone capable of giving with more purpose, care, and connection. Gifting has never been about the occasion. It's about the giftee.- the giftee matters most.

The most powerful shift you can make is this:

👉 Prioritize the giftee.

👉 Present gifts that spark joy, stir memory, or speak to the soul.

👉 Practice being an intentional gifter.

You may already be an intentional gifter. For some it is in your DNA. For others it's right on the surface. And then there are folks who have to work harder, but it's there deep down. And with TTE, thought, time and effort, you'll uncover it and grow it with every gift you give.

🖌️ Reflection Prompt

How do you see yourself as a gifter right now?

Be honest. Do you give from habit, or from heart? From pressure or from presence? Burnt out from giving?

Your answer is the starting point, and we'll build from here.

Reflect_____

_____

_____

_____

_____

_____

_____

23

a little about me...

Hi, I'm Gina Carrell and if you've ever asked me what my dream job is, you probably heard me say: "If I could wake up every day and do exactly what I love, I'd be a professional gift giver." What I affectionately termed a gifter.

Some people think well that's fun, others think it's a little weird. But in my closest circle, they believed I could turn my dream into something real. Now what that looked like, no one knew. This is my first step.

I'm a gifter at heart. I find joy in celebrating with others with meaning and care. I love curating thoughtful gifts that make people feel seen, loved, and appreciated. Receiving gifts is one of the five love languages. So, what better way to express care than gifts?

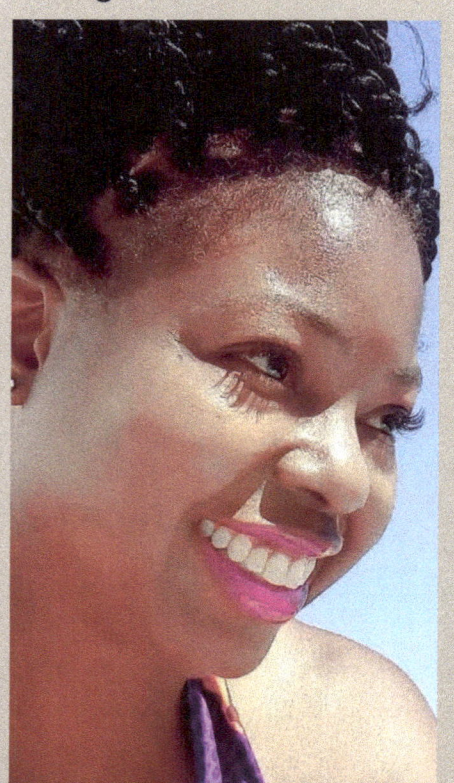

I'm a wife, mom, sister, daughter, friend, cousin, frequent flyer of all airlines, foodie, baby yogi, and a volunteer in my community, who also serves in the military. I'm native to Myrtle Beach, SC, but currently call the DMV my home.

In all of my roles, I try to live with intention, to find the good, to lead with compassion, and to create meaningful moments wherever I can.

Writing this guide has been a labor of love, and my hope is that it helps you see gifting, not as a task or checking the box, but as an opportunity to connect deeply with the people who matter most.

Thanks for being here with me. Let's make gifting more joyful together.

Intentional Gifter: IG/TikTok/FB page
www.intentionalgifter.com